I have seen firsthand, on a professional and personal level, Ben Trueblood's passion for God and students. Ben was on our staff and student pastor to my sons. His experience in the local church and at LifeWay provides unique and much needed insight on having a healthy student ministry. When I started in ministry as a student pastor, I could only wish such a resource existed. It is long overdue and I highly recommend it to you.

Dr. Grant Ethridge, senior pastor,
Liberty Baptist Church, Hampton, VA

It's possible to look healthy on the outside, but be slowly dying on the inside, especially in ministry. Research, statisticians, and socialists continue to reveal the fracture between this generation and the local church. It feels that no ground has been gained in an effort to keep our students connected to the local church after high school despite our conferences, camps, and events. Could it be that we have been asking the wrong questions such as "does it work" versus "will it last"? Ben Trueblood addresses this pertinent dilemma head-on with a masterful, all-encompassing, wholistic approach to reshape student ministry to once more see life change take place for kingdom impact. Let me assure you these principles shared are not formulas or techniques, but instead biblical building blocks that will create a solidified, wholistic student ministry that will stand the test of time and trends.

Ed Newton, lead pastor,
Community Bible Church, San Antonio, TX

Ben Trueblood's heart for student ministry can be seen throughout this book, *Student Ministry That Matters*. This book focuses on the things that will bring eternal impact in the lives of students and their families. Do not get distracted by the peripherals, but focus on these elements laid out in his book to lead a healthy student ministry.

Dr. Jonathan Geukgeuzian, executive director of the Center for Youth Ministries Christian Leadership & Church Ministries Chair, School of Divinity, Liberty University

Ben Trueblood is a great friend and significant thought-leader for those who care deeply about student ministry. *Student Ministry That Matters* breaks through the airwaves that are filled with white noise concerning best strategies and best practices. While this resource is not a magic formula offering instant success, such a resource has yet to be created, Ben has articulated a biblically informed understanding of health in any student ministry no matter the size, strategy, or denomination. This book allows one to rethink student ministry with a sacred simplicity that is *Kingdom Expanding*, *Character Transforming*, and *Culture Shaping*.

Brent Crowe, Ph.D., vice president, Student Leadership University

To be honest, I was just planning to scan the book *Student Ministry That Matters*. But that proved impossible. Ben Trueblood's writing pulled me in and I read every line. Content to allow other books to present specific student ministry strategies, Ben gives all his attention to those three elements that should drive all we do with and for teenagers. He calls for ministry that is *Kingdom Expanding* (accelerating the number of those who experience salvation), *Character Transforming* (shaping a student's character through the life-giving power and freedom of the gospel found by knowing Jesus through His Word), and *Culture Shaping* (students shaping the beliefs, values, and way of life for the people around them). Student ministries that keep these three elements paramount will see Christ's kingdom come on earth.

Richard Ross, Ph.D., professor of Student Ministry, Southwestern Seminary

Ben Trueblood has the knowledge and wisdom to guide student pastors and leaders to have a thriving ministry that makes a difference in this world. His anointing and tenure in student ministry has led him to write *Student Ministry That Matters*. It should be on the must-read list for those who want to implement a healthy student ministry that makes a real difference for the kingdom, and that helps change students lives, for the rest of their lives.

Wade Morris, itinerant minister, evangelist, founder of Journey Bible Study Series

I don't say this flippantly: Ben has written a masterpiece here, and not because he's saying anything new or edgy. He's putting basic truths of youth ministry in plain, tangible form for those of us who are called to evangelize and disciple students. This book is readable and practical, but it's also do-able. You can read this on your own or with your team of volunteers, staff, parents, and interns. What a gift to the church.

Clayton King, evangelist, pastor, and author of *True Love Project*

978-1-4336-4449-8

Published by B&H Publishing Group
Nashville, Tennessee

Dewey Decimal Classification: 259
Subject Heading: Ministers of Youth \ Youth \
Church Work with Youth

1 2 3 4 5 6 • 21 20 19 18 17 16

STUDENT MINISTRY

—— THAT ——

MATTERS

3 ELEMENTS OF A HEALTHY STUDENT MINISTRY

BEN TRUEBLOOD

PUBLISHING GROUP

NASHVILLE, TENNESSEE

For Kristen, whose unwavering and Christlike love through the years makes me stand in awe. And for Jonathan, Avery, Josiah, and Adrienne, who are each a blessing from the Lord in their own unique way.

Contents

Kingdom Expanding

Character Transforming

Culture Shaping

Acknowledgments

I WANT TO THANK FORMER PASTORS DR. RONNIE FLOYD AND DR. BUDDY Gray for giving me the opportunity to serve in student ministry on each of your teams. To Dr. Floyd, thank you for challenging me beyond my comfort zone and rooting my early ministry in the accomplishment of the Great Commission. To Buddy, thank you for challenging me theologically and for leading me to an expanded view of God that has distinctly marked my ministry. It was an honor to serve with you both.

Pastor Grant Ethridge, thank you for believing in me and giving me so many leadership opportunities. Thank you for personally investing in me as my pastor. Serving with you will always be one of the greatest joys of my life. It was an honor to serve with you, and it is an honor to call you friend.

To my team at LifeWay Student Ministry, you are an amazingly gifted team that God has brought together to serve His church in their mission of making disciples. Thank you for your passion for the Lord, for student ministry leaders, and for students. Your impact in the discipleship of teenagers throughout the world reaches far beyond what you get to see. I'm proud to work alongside you.

Thank you, Dad, for your unceasing prayers for my family and me. Thank you for living for Jesus in front of me each day. Your discipling influence in my life has had a profound impact on me and my ministry that continues to this day. You're my hero.

Kristen, you're the best.

Foreword

SADLY, IN SOME CHURCHES AND IN SOME STUDENT MINISTRIES, LEO Tolstoy would be viewed as a hero, a model for moral discipline and Christian virtue. Tolstoy was a famous Russian philosopher and author in the mid-1800s, best known for his novel *War and Peace*. He pursued moralistic perfection in his faith, a task that many viewed as noble. He set up lengthy and complex lists of rules for himself and trusted those lists to guide his life, even forming rules for controlling his emotions. Several times, he publicly vowed to be celibate—though he was married—so he ended up living in a separate bedroom from his wife.

Despite all of his attempts and his public commitments, Tolstoy could never live up to his own standards. His wife's sixteen pregnancies were a reminder of his inability to keep his vow of celibacy. A. W. Wilson, a Tolstoy biographer, wrote: "Tolstoy suffered from a fundamental theological inability to understand the Incarnation. His religion was a thing of Law rather than a thing of Grace, a scheme for human betterment rather than a vision for God penetrating a fallen world."[1]

Tolstoy pursued perfection in his own strength and energy apart from the grace of God. He constantly lived under guilt and shame, and he died a miserable vagrant. He never enjoyed the Christian life because he missed the essence of Christianity. As John Stott stated, "The essence of sin is man substituting himself for God, while the essence of salvation is God substituting himself for man."[2] The essence of the Christian faith is God taking our place, not only on the cross but also as the One who daily sustains and satisfies us. Tolstoy, because he missed grace, lived the antithesis of the Christian faith.

Sadly, some churches want their student ministries to be production centers for students to be like Leo Tolstoy. Student ministries can drift away from the grace of God and drift into morality training, burdening students and parents with virtues apart from the Vine. Students, indeed all of us, are incapable of living the Christian life in our own merit. We are utterly unable to transform ourselves. Because of this simple truth, transformation is not about trying; it is about dying. The apostle Paul knew that transformation occurs when we continually die to ourselves and trust the grace of Christ fully: "For we who live are always being given over to death for Jesus' sake, so that the life of Jesus also may be manifested in our mortal flesh" (2 Cor. 4:11 ESV).

In this book, Ben Trueblood articulates that student ministry must be about character transformation, not mere character formation. This is because our character does not need mere improvement. It needs transformation. And when the hearts of students are transformed, the kingdom is expanded and the culture is shaped.

I have heard Ben passionately speak about these elements in student ministry. I have seen him train student pastors on these elements and watched him make ministry decisions based on the conviction that any healthy student ministry is going to aggressively go after heart and character transformation.

Ben writes from experience and with hands that are still very active in local church student ministry. Though he leads a large team of student ministry leaders who create resources and provide events for teenagers, he still serves students as a "Sunday school teacher" for high school guys. He has street cred. He is not just talking student discipleship; he is discipling students.

Like Ben, I "cut my teeth" in student ministry. I loved it, mainly because I saw the deep impact ministry to students has on the trajectory of a teenager. I still love it, and I am very grateful for those who serve students. They are heroes. If you are serving students, thank you! Thank you for your investment.

I hired Ben at LifeWay from a local church student ministry role. He was and is well respected among his peers for his passion and ability to disciple students, develop them as leaders, and deploy them on mission. If today is like every other day, Ben woke up today thinking about making disciples in a student ministry context. You will benefit from what he has learned.

Eric Geiger

VP, LifeWay Christian Resources, Nashville, Tennessee

Introduction

IS MY STUDENT MINISTRY HEALTHY? THIS IS A QUESTION THAT I'VE asked countless times. It's a question that has brought me to both anger and tears. I will never forget sitting in my boss's office as an associate student pastor when the anger and tears finally collided. We were talking about the state of the ministry and what we needed to do next. We were growing in numbers, but something just didn't feel right. It didn't feel healthy. It was at this point that years of this question exploded into a "there must be more to student ministry than this" moment. There were loud voices, frustrated tears, and I will admit a bit of inexcusable immature behavior on my part.

This conversation changed me. It launched me out of a number-focused approach to ministry and onto a journey to discover what it looked like to have a healthy student ministry. God began to bring Scripture, experiences, and people into my life over the next decade plus that would continue to shape this picture of student ministry health.

Two people I would like to thank specifically are Grant Ethridge and Eric Geiger. Pastor Grant gave me the opportunity and freedom to lead a student ministry focused on health, and Eric refined language that articulated thoughts and practices that had been bouncing around in my head for the last ten years.

What you won't find in this book is a new ministry strategy. There are plenty of those books out there already. As far as strategy is concerned, I would encourage you to think through your own ministry strategy through the lens of your church context and what God has called you to do in ministry. He has shaped you and gifted you uniquely for your church and your students.

Think about this for a moment: you have been appointed by God to shepherd the exact students who are in your ministry. And they have been appointed to you. Yes, the squirrelly sixth grader who steals your phone and changes the language to Portuguese at every opportunity. Yes, the ones who don't seem to care about anything. Yes, the ones who show up because their parents make them. Yes, the ones who are not yet part of your ministry. God has appointed you to them and them to you, and He has gifted you to minister to them. If He has done all of this, then He can give you wisdom to develop a strategy that is unique, personal, and the perfect fit for the context in which He has placed you.

What you are going to find in this book is the answer to the question that haunted me for so many years in student ministry: "Is my student ministry healthy?"

Regardless of your ministry context, church size, denomination, or years of experience, it is possible for you to have a healthy student ministry. The three elements explained throughout the rest of this book will lead you to that very thing. Will this book stop you from asking the question, "Is my student ministry healthy?" I hope not. What this book will do is give you, and your leaders, a framework to answer this question and will help you highlight areas of improvement as you seek to lead a student ministry focused on health.

Discussion Questions

1. Is my student ministry healthy?

2. What do you hope to accomplish from reading this book?

3. What are all the implications of being a shepherd over the students in your ministry or small group?

Chapter 1

The Three Elements of a Healthy Student Ministry

IN THE 2004 ATHENS OLYMPIC GAMES MATT EMMONS, AMERICAN SPORT shooter, was on his way to his second gold medal of the games. He needed to post a score of 7.2 in order to take home the gold, and his lowest score to that point was a 9.3. He had it in the bag. As he took aim on his last shot, he pulled the trigger and recorded a perfect bull's-eye. The only problem was that the target he hit was not the target in his designated lane. Matt's bull's-eye was on the wrong target, and instead of claiming his second gold medal of the games he slipped to eighth place in the event.

In order to have a healthy student ministry, you need to be aimed at the right target. My hope for this book is to give you the target that can help you win. Regardless of where you fall on the student ministry leader spectrum—volunteer, part-time, or full-time—you can aim at this target and have a healthy ministry where students and their families become lifelong disciples of Jesus.

That is the win, isn't it? Not to see students change for a short time, but to actually see them living for Jesus for the rest of their lives. You can see this begin to happen in the small group you lead, in the class you teach, or in the student ministry you lead.

Your target for a healthy student ministry consists of three areas I will refer to as "elements."

The three elements of a healthy student ministry that you will engage with throughout this book are extremely important because they will help you fulfill the calling that God has placed on your life to serve in student ministry. Seeing student ministry through the lens of these three elements will help you keep your eyes, and your work, focused on long-term health rather than on the many shortcuts that give the illusion of health. Many believe that student ministry is about having more students at "X" than they had last year.

This is a dangerous belief because it can cause you as a student leader to see student ministry as a formula rather than a disciple-making organism. Formulaic student ministry says, "I know if I do these eight things, then I will have more students than I did last time." Student ministry in this context is reduced to the execution of a playbook rather than reliance upon God to reveal vision, direction, and clarity to an ever-changing and living organism.

This is one reason why it's important to understand that the three elements you will find in this book are not just another ministry strategy or formula. They are specific enough to provide direct application, yet general enough for you to be able to fit them into your own ministry context. As your ministry strategies change and adjust to the ever-changing world of student ministry, this is a target that will remain constant for you.

All three ministry elements are necessary because you can't have a healthy student ministry without all three being present and working together. At this point you may be skeptical. "Did he really say a ministry couldn't be healthy without these three elements?" I believe that strongly because I've seen it work. I've led in student ministry according to these three elements (using different language, but the same principles) and have seen a ministry turn from unhealthy and dysfunctional to healthy and thriving. We experienced both explosive growth and steadily climbing growth. We saw students come to know Jesus and students surrender their lives to missions and ministry. The ministry is still growing and thriving long after I've been gone.

This didn't happen because of me, or my team of staff and volunteers, even though they were awesome and we worked extremely hard. It happened because God blessed the ministry when we were aiming at the right target. We're not the only ministry to experience what it's like to be part of a healthy student ministry. As I've talked with thousands of student pastors and volunteers over the past few years, these three elements have continued to rise to the top as the driving factors influencing student ministry health. With these three elements as your target, you will have a healthy student ministry. It will only be a matter of time.

So what are the three ministry elements?

They are:

1. Kingdom Expanding
2. Character Transforming
3. Culture Shaping

What I found on my personal journey to leading a healthy student ministry was that it's the basic things that are often overlooked yet are the most important. In student ministry it's easy to get lost in the hype and activity. If you get stuck here, it is the quickest off-ramp on the road to student ministry health. Steve Jobs, former co-founder and CEO of Apple, was known for his commitment to focus and simplicity. He said, "Simplicity can be harder than complex: You have to work hard to get your thinking clean to make it simple. But it's worth it in the end because once you get there, you can move mountains."[3]

The way that you move mountains in student ministry is by mobilizing a team of people around a simple idea that they can easily articulate to you and to each other. Remember that whatever level of leadership you have in student ministry, you are a leader of other people. Student ministry isn't meant to be done in isolation. Because of this, it isn't enough that you alone are aimed at the right target. You need to ensure that your students, volunteers, and staff team are aimed at the right target as well. That kind of synergy doesn't come from complexity or a clever gimmick. The three elements become the tool of simplicity that can help you lead your student ministry to a place of greater health and effectiveness.

As a side note, if you aren't reading this with your volunteer team, I highly recommend that you do. A healthy student ministry isn't led by one person, but by a team of people who all desire a healthy student ministry and know how to get there together. There will be questions at the end of each chapter moving forward that will help you guide discussion with your leaders as you enter into this journey together. There is great power in your ministry when you as an entire student ministry team operate together as one body with the same language.

Discussion Questions

1. At this time, is there one element that our ministry does better than the others?

2. Is our ministry currently structured for short-term results or long-term health?

3. Are there moments in the recent past when we have become stuck in the hype and activity of student ministry? How can we move more toward simplicity?

Kingdom Expanding

Chapter 2

Element #1:
Kingdom Expanding

HEALTHY STUDENT MINISTRIES ARE *KINGDOM EXPANDING*. THEY ARE evangelistic. In a healthy student ministry there will be students who meet Jesus and are rescued from their sin. You've heard this statement before: "The majority of people who meet Jesus do so before the age of eighteen." It's heard so frequently that for many it's become cliché and even ignored. This is unacceptable. The reality of student ministry is that you are called to one of the most fertile mission fields in the world as you minister to students and their families, and evangelizing this mission field is directly linked to the overall health of your student ministry.

I learned early on in student ministry that words have to be defined. Students need to know what you mean when you use words like *evangelism, sin, discipleship,* and *God's Kingdom.* It is in that spirit that I want to help you with some definitions related to this element. When I refer to "Kingdom" here, I am referring to God's Kingdom of people who have placed their faith in Him. Others have called it the universal church. In its most basic definition it simply means all believers everywhere. To expand God's Kingdom then means that your student ministry will be involved in adding people to God's Kingdom.

Throughout history this process has been closely linked to evangelism. In the Bible evangelism is presented in terms of giftedness (Eph. 4:11) and as an instruction for all believers (Matt. 28:19). It's important to note that while God gifts some people more than others in this area, not having this giftedness doesn't remove us from the responsibility of being evangelistic in both our personal lives and as leaders of student ministry.

The very definition of evangelism lends itself to both a leadership form as well as a personal form: evangelism is the spreading of the gospel through public preaching or personal witness.

For a student ministry to truly embody this element, it must fulfill both aspects of this definition. A healthy student ministry will share the gospel through its preaching as well as train its people to share the gospel in a personal setting, which we will talk about more in the next few chapters. As the story of Jesus is shared in these public and private moments, people will have an opportunity to respond to that message by placing their faith in Jesus. Through the work of the Holy Spirit and this action of faith, people are added to God's Kingdom. Being a *Kingdom Expanding* ministry cannot happen if the ministry is not evangelistic. There's only one problem: student ministries in general are far less evangelistic than in years past.

I've noticed throughout the years that student pastors have developed adverse feelings to the following words: *evangelist, evangelistic, numbers,* and *invitation.* At the same time churches in the Southern Baptist Convention have declined in youth baptisms at an alarming rate. In 2013 60 percent of the 46,125 SBC churches reported not baptizing a single person ages 12 to 17. In order to be in the top 100 list of SBC churches in youth baptisms, a church needs only to baptize 36 teenagers. Since the year 2000 total annual youth baptisms (ages 12 to 17) in the SBC decreased from 93,100 to 71,457 in 2014. Student ministries are not reaching the youth of our nation effectively.

Healthy student ministries are evangelistic, but they aren't manipulative with the gospel. There are two contributing factors to the adverse feelings toward *evangelist, evangelistic, numbers,* and *invitation.* First, there has been a reaction to what many would label as an unhealthy approach to evangelism that was present in student ministry in the 1990s and early 2000s. Many leaders will remember a time when an emotionally charged message lacking a strong biblical foundation would be given with a vague (and again, emotional) invitation plea encouraging everyone in the crowd to come to the altar and make a decision.

Second, we have a more theologically aware and diverse group of student ministry leaders in today's culture. There are more theological conversations happening between student pastors, leaders, and students now than ever before, especially related to topics in the Reformed tradition. These two factors have caused the pendulum to swing in student ministry, and it needed to. The unintended result is that the pendulum has now swung to a place with devastating consequences.

As a student pastor, I remember one sermon more than any other. I invited someone to speak at an event for our students, and he preached one of the greatest messages I had ever heard in my life. The guest preacher traced Jesus throughout all of Scripture over the course of about fifty minutes with my students. Yes, it was fifty minutes, and they were engaged the entire time. The preacher was dynamic and clear in his delivery, but my students were absolutely captivated by Jesus as they encountered Him throughout all of Scripture and saw how the Bible, collectively, is the story of God's plan to redeem His people. "Light bulbs" were going off in students' minds all over the room. It was an amazing moment.

Then we got to the end of the message.

After spending fifty minutes brilliantly walking students through the gospel of Jesus throughout the Bible, the message ended with a prayer and an amen. There was no action step. There was no invitation. There was no public opportunity given for students to respond to the grace of God they had just been exposed to. I will remember that moment for the rest of my life.

Instead of correcting the evangelistic course of student ministry, many leaders have allowed a theological position or a disdain for past events (perhaps both) to keep them from fully accomplishing the Great Commission (Matt. 28:18–20). A student ministry cannot be healthy if it isn't expanding God's Kingdom. Student pastors and leaders must return to an evangelistic mind-set, but not one characterized by the mistakes of our past. *Kingdom Expanding* evangelism is much more than convincing students to pray a prayer or come forward the last night of camp. *Kingdom Expanding* evangelism ensures that students understand the gospel and the reality that God invites us to respond to His grace. Because of this, student ministry leaders must consistently provide opportunities for students to respond to the gospel. Giving an invitation isn't manipulative, and thinking evangelistically doesn't mean you're all about the numbers.

Thinking evangelistically in its simplest form means that you as a student ministry leader will find a way to connect students to the gospel in everything you do. As an evangelistically thinking leader you will constantly ask the following question: "How does this connect students to the gospel?" Ask this question throughout the planning phase of an event and use it as a point of evaluation for every event and ongoing program that takes place throughout the ministry.

Ministries that are truly *Kingdom Expanding* will be willing to remove or reengineer events and programs that don't line up with their mission. Evangelistically thinking leaders will also train their volunteer teams to think evangelistically. Not only will that evaluative question be in your mind as the student pastor, it should also be in the mind of every volunteer on your team. This takes constant and unending communication. Until your leaders begin using this question to evaluate their own role and you hear it in conversation with you and between other leaders, it hasn't taken root. There are many things you can (and should) delegate as a leader, but driving a heart for *Kingdom Expansion* deeply within your team is not one of them. It is priority one for you in your effort to lead a healthy student ministry. Being a *Kingdom Expanding* ministry cannot be done as an afterthought.

The road to health begins as you embrace building a student ministry that is *Kingdom Expanding*. We are in a time when student ministry desperately needs pastors and leaders who will return to an evangelistic mind-set that is centered on the gospel of Jesus Christ because it alone is has the power to save all who believe (Rom. 1:16).

Discussion Questions

1. How effective is our ministry at expanding God's Kingdom?

2. What does it mean to be evangelistic?

3. Knowing the current state of evangelism, what can our ministry do now to reach more students with the gospel?

Chapter 3

Kingdom Expansion Modeled by the Leader

AS AN EIGHTH AND NINTH GRADER I WAS LOST, BUT VERY RELIGIOUS and very involved in the student ministry at my church in Springdale, Arkansas. I was the student who placed my faith in Christ as a senior in high school and everyone thought, "I thought he was already saved." You know the ones; you've had kids like me in your own ministry as well. In those early years as a student in the ministry, I remember vividly the student ministry staff at the time (an intern and youth pastor) taking me and a few others on Saturdays in the summer to people's houses to thank them for visiting our church and to tell them about Jesus. Some of you will recognize this process under the term *visitation* while others of you will see this as the most foreign thing that could ever be done. "You actually visited people at their houses? That's crazy!" Well, we did it, and it worked.

It worked in that we saw people come to faith in Christ, and it worked in that it forced me into a situation that I wasn't comfortable with at all: sharing Jesus one-on-one with someone. I watched as the gospel was shared from house to house, and all I really had to do was introduce myself. "This is going pretty well," I thought. Then we got to the house where our leader looked at the student standing in the doorway and said, "This is Ben, and he has something he would like to share with you." I was scared to death, and to this day I wish I could have seen my face in that moment. I stumbled through what I had heard presented at the last few houses as quickly as I could and as best I could remember.

Maybe they saw something in me, maybe they thought of me as a leader, maybe I was just one of the only ones who would go. I'm not sure of any of that, but I know that they thought enough of me to invest in me. Their plan was a strategic one, though I didn't see it at the time; their plan was to instill in my life the skill and in my heart a desire to share Jesus with people.

Fast-forward to years later. I was able to do this very thing with students in my own ministry, and I finally got to see the look of fear that was probably on my face all those years ago as it was plastered on the face of the student standing next to me. I remember a lot about those days as a student, but one of the things I remember most is the deeply rooted passion of a student ministry intern and a high school pastor to share the gospel, to expand God's Kingdom.

For a student ministry to be *Kingdom Expanding* it must be in the heart of the leader. If seeing people come to know Christ isn't one of the greatest joys of your life personally, then it will never be one of the greatest joys of your ministry as a whole. For a ministry to be *Kingdom Expanding*, the gospel needs to be present off the stage as well as on it. It's easy for a student ministry leader to be passionate about students being passionate about the gospel. We have plenty of that. What we lack is leaders who themselves, in their personal lives, are passionate about the gospel. I wish that, as a student pastor, I would've taken more students to more houses to teach them how to share their faith. I wish that I could tell you this was a constant part of my ministry that defined who we were, rather than the reality that it was a practice done in seasons and on trips.

Your ministry is on the road to health when your students begin to think more evangelistically. This is something that is caught and taught, but too often our ministries just focus on the "taught" side of things. Students need to see healthy evangelism modeled as well. They will focus on what they see you doing far more than what they hear you saying. You know as well as I do that one of the ways to begin effectively reaching students again in our nation is to train an army of students to reach their friends, their neighborhoods, and their school campuses. It will not happen through a more creative event than you did last year, or through the sixteen hours you spent preparing your sermon this week. Those things are important in ministry, but they can't turn the tide on their own.

What would your ministry, community, and church look like if you mobilized your team of student ministry leaders on a consistent basis to train students to think about all areas of life through a *Kingdom Expanding* filter and then help them put into practice the sharing of their faith? Students need to be taught how to use their talents and abilities as a platform for the gospel. They need to have their eyes opened to the truth that their teams, squads, homes, and clubs are their closest and most accessible mission fields. A ministry *becomes a Kingdom Expanding ministry when students become Kingdom Expanding* students. In order for that to happen your students need to see that your life, the lives of your staff team, and the lives of your volunteer team are about making disciples in the strength and power of Christ (Col. 1:11).

Discussion Questions

1. Are we modeling the level of evangelism we want to see in our students?

2. What are some things we can do to begin training students to share their faith?

3. Do our current students see their teams, clubs, etc., as mission fields? What can we do to support the students in these areas specifically?

Chapter 4

Kingdom Expansion Is More Than Church Expansion

FOR THE LAST THREE YEARS AS I'VE LED THE STUDENT TEAM FOR LifeWay, I've had the privilege of personally interacting with hundreds of churches of various sizes and contexts. These interactions have confirmed what I've known in my heart for a long time: *the size of your ministry doesn't determine the health of your ministry.*

I've encountered small student ministries that were incredibly healthy and large ones that were dysfunctional. The opposite has also been true. Student ministry is about more than just drawing a crowd or growing your group.

Before we get too far, let me be clear about something: this is not an anti-numbers manifesto. I believe in tracking numbers, setting goals, and having a level of accountability associated with them. I also understand that there is a fear associated with numeric measurement in the church that leads student pastors to frustration in ministry, constant church hopping to find the perfect numberless place, or to quit the ministry altogether. Goals and accountability are a necessity of ministry, not an evil. However, frustration sets in if the focus on numeric measures becomes imbalanced.

There are a couple of thoughts that drive this fear of numeric measure. The first of these is that it takes the focus off ministry and people. This is true only if you let it happen. Even in an intense, pressure-filled situation, you control whether or not the numeric measures pull your eyes off ministry and people. You control that, not the people above you in the leadership chain.

I can remember the exact moment when this fear became a reality for me. I allowed the numbers and the pressure to take my focus off the ministry and the people. I didn't know what was going on at the time, but I felt the frustration that came as a result. Years later, as I looked back at that situation, I began to see that the imbalance wasn't in the church or in those leading me. It was in me.

What I came to understand out of making this error is the pressure you feel from numeric measurement will only change the way you do ministry if you let it. If God has put a specific vision in you for ministry, then you can't allow the fear of measurement to knock you off course. Your reaction to pressure is your choice.

A second thought that drives this fear is when we measure numerically we are measuring something we don't have direct control over. The primary argument here is that God is the one who "brings the increase," not the minister. I completely agree.

God is the one who brings the increase; and a person is not going to be saved, baptized, attend a group, grow in their faith, or anything else without God doing a work in their life. One problem related to this is when a lazy minister tries to hide behind this truth as an excuse. God has put you in that ministry position for a reason, and the expectation is that we would work hard to accomplish the assignment He has given. In Psalm 90:17 we see Moses exclaiming for God to establish the work of their hands. The assumption is that Moses and the people were working hard while at the same time he understood that for any of it to be effective the Lord would have to establish that work. When you have a balanced view on this topic, numeric measures can help you identify areas where you need to improve in order to fulfill the calling He has placed on your life.

Still, there is a very real temptation in student ministry to focus solely on *church* expansion rather than *kingdom* expansion. There is a distinct difference. A church-expanding mindset will only care about getting students in the door or at the event. They will only care about the end result of the event in an attendance or decision count. A *Kingdom Expanding* ministry will care about getting people in the door and the decision count, but they will also care about what happens to the students after the event is over. Unfortunately, this is a missing component in many student ministries today.

A truly *Kingdom Expanding* ministry will make sure that students understand the gospel and will help them connect to the ministry as a whole where they can begin the discipleship process. This is what God commands us to do in the entirety of the Great Commission. There is a conversion moment as well as a continued discipleship element. It's true that you can't have the discipleship element if there's no conversion. However, a student ministry will be dysfunctional if event after event produces spiritual orphans who don't understand what to do next and have nowhere to go. Student pastors and leaders, your job isn't finished at the moment of decision.

One of the biggest attacks of the Enemy is to get you as the leader to begin placing your worth and value in the results of your ministry, to get you thinking church expansion only. I've been in that dark place. There was a time in my own ministry when I would evaluate and judge my performance based on the number of decisions made at the end of a message or the number of people who showed up to an event. It took the wise words of a mentor to reveal to me my pride in that thought process. Through his intervention I came to understand that if I'm going to blame myself when things in ministry don't go the right way, then there will be something inside me that will take credit for ministry successes. Both directions are deadly to ministry leadership.

The way to combat this temptation is to stay vigilantly focused on *Kingdom Expansion* and to put the "work of your hands" into the things God has placed in front of you. I've found consistently in student ministry that if I'm faithful to the gospel and leading students to it, God will take care of the growth part Himself. After all, He is much better at growing things than I am.

Discussion Questions

1. Are we allowing numerical measurement to define our identities as student ministry leaders or define the health of our ministry?

2. What are some goals that we can set in our ministry that are balanced and will help lead us to growth?

3. As we've seen, prayer is a major component in staying on course with this element. Pause now and spend time praying that God would protect you and your team from pride, that He would give you a healthy ministry, and that He would bless the work of your hands and your labor.

Chapter 5

Kingdom Expansion Is More Than a Service Project

KINGDOM EXPANDING STUDENT MINISTRIES HELP THEIR STUDENTS SEE and connect with God's heart for the nations. God's heart for the nations is clear throughout Scripture. It's seen through His interactions with His people, His plan for salvation, and His commands for us to continue sharing the gospel story. When students leave our ministries, we need to make sure that they see beyond our towns and cities. We need to help them engage in taking the gospel to the nations early and often.

Special emphasis on social justice among Christians in recent years has made a significant impact on this generation of students, and not just the ones from your church. Now, more than ever before, students are ready to get involved in things they feel are making a difference in the world. From the coffee you choose to drink, to the shoes you choose to wear, to posting a selfie with a red "X" on your hand, the options to be socially aware and involved are simple and plentiful. The impact has also been felt among students in the church through a renewed eagerness to serve their communities and get involved in missions. With all the positive impact this social justice awareness boom has brought, it has also brought some challenges for you as a leader.

Primarily, this challenge is to keep the gospel central in missions. We are at a place where missions and the Great Commission must be redefined for your students. It would be a failure of epic proportions for students to grow up in our ministries and believe that they can fulfill the Great Commission without the message ever being shared or to believe that missions is the same as buying shoes or coffee or writing a red "X" on their hand.

Romans 10 reveals the necessity of a gospel messenger and the importance of the message being shared. I encourage you to read it, but here are some main points:

1. Everyone who calls on the name of the Lord will be saved.
2. To call on the Lord, a person must believe.
3. For one to believe, they have to get the message.
4. For someone to get the message, there needs to be a messenger.
5. The messenger shares the message of Christ.

Other key passages that you are familiar with related to missions (Ps. 96:3; Matt. 28:19–20; Acts 1:8) all point to the message being shared, proclaimed, declared—you get the idea. It's important for your students to have opportunities to serve, but that service isn't missions unless the gospel is shared.

Through my role with LifeWay Students I have the privilege of working with a missions ministry called World Changers. The purpose of World Changers is to share the gospel through construction-based ministry. Notice the language and structure of their purpose: it is first and foremost to share the gospel, not to do construction. The construction project is the avenue that gets students in a place to share the gospel.

This isn't the way it has always been. When I first arrived at LifeWay in the spring of 2012, many saw World Changers as a ministry focused more on construction than on sharing the gospel. Far too often, construction projects were considered a success whether the gospel was shared or not. Sometimes students were told to get back to work instead of allowing them to share the gospel in the neighborhood. Many times the homeowners where the work was taking place weren't even engaged in conversation. Certainly there were coordinators, church leaders, and teenagers focused on sharing the gospel in those days, but they seemed to be more the exception than the rule.

Too many leaders made World Changers all about the construction work and exposing students to hard work and service while the gospel had taken a backseat. But even for these leaders, I don't believe this was done on purpose. Such a subtle shift in focus is an example of how quickly *Kingdom Expansion* can slip away without constant attention.

Over the last three years our World Changers team has worked hard to fix this. They've reorganized projects, retrained staff and volunteers, and have made difficult decisions to bring the ministry to a place where it truly is "gospel sharing through construction-based ministry." In the summer of 2015 alone, students in World Changers cities shared the gospel 19,408 times, and 568 people in those cities placed their faith in Jesus.

Yes, we are called to clothe the naked, feed the hungry, take care of the orphans and widows, work to abolish sex trafficking, and much more. As the church we should be leading the way. We must also be gospel focused in our efforts. There's too much at stake to allow the cultural focus on meeting social needs to steer us away from the reason we are to meet social needs in the first place: to take the gospel to the ends of the earth. At this point I think it's important to recognize that there will be times when you won't be able to share the gospel message because of the situation. For example, in a church planting or international missions experience you may not be able to share the gospel with each person you come in contact with, or even on an entire trip, but the way that you serve people will lay the foundation for the gospel to be shared by the local church when barriers can be overcome.

There is something special that happens in the life of a student (or any person) when they make the connection between meeting physical needs and sharing the gospel for salvation, and part of your role as a leader of students is to bring this connection to life. If our missions efforts are not leading students to make this connection, then we are missing the mark.

Discussion Questions

1. What are some areas of need around our community where we can make an impact?

2. How can we make sure the gospel remains at the center of our community ministry efforts?

3. What are some of the issues of our day that our students want to engage with? How can we help them get involved?

Character Transforming

Chapter 6

Element #2: Character Transforming

I SPENT THE FIRST THREE YEARS OF COLLEGE IN THE BUSINESS SCHOOL at the University of Arkansas where the focus of my degree was transportation and logistics. Many of our discussions focused on Walmart, which isn't surprising considering Walmart's headquarters is nearby and the business school is named after its founder, Sam Walton.

The bulk of our study of Walmart centered on their vast distribution network and technologically advanced distribution centers. It is an incredible thing to see this massive web of conveyer belts at work. At that time they could do things that no other company could do because of the efficiencies their distribution system allowed them to accomplish. This distribution system was a main driver in their ability to expand into new areas quickly as well as keep their prices lower than most competitors because they were able to get products from manufacturers to the store shelves at an incredible speed. This is a great way to do business, but it is not a great way to do student ministry. Yet there are many who approach student ministry with a similar mind-set—a conveyer belt production mentality.

A common approach to student ministry is to say, "When my students graduate and leave for college, what do I want them to look like?" This question sounds great. I love the forward-thinking aspect of it. But the unintended consequence of this question is that our student ministries look more like a distribution system of conveyer belts made to form the character of a student rather than a place that nurtures a living organism and where Jesus freely works in the lives of students on an individual basis.

In order to create the desired college freshman, we back up and establish a list of what students need to do and what they need to avoid doing. From there the belief is if a sixth grader is placed on the ministry conveyer belt (and they stick with the process), by the time they graduate they will know how to be good Christian boys and girls. Only, creating good Christian boys and girls isn't the goal of a student ministry. "Good Christians" are produced by constantly feeding students information about what they should and shouldn't do. It's creating for them a list that they can complete, and when they complete the list they look good and it makes the leader feel successful.

The unfortunate part of this is that they'll never be able to complete the list, which only leads them to a life of spiritual failure and spiritual depression. Why? Because they are led to an impossible standard of living instead of being led to Christ. This model of student ministry teaches them to trust in themselves and what they can accomplish rather than to trust in what Jesus has accomplished for them.

I am not advocating the abandonment of the commands that God has clearly given that our students need to know. What I am advocating is that healthy student ministries make an intentional shift to apply these truths through the lens of the gospel. There are three ways you can do this.

First, help students develop an understanding of their sin. This is especially true for ones who placed their faith in Jesus at an early age. Sadly, many (among adults as well) forget what it was like to be rescued from their sin. A reality for students is that they will never understand the depth of their salvation if they don't understand the depth of their sin. As I speak in student ministries across the country, I am constantly reminded that students don't know what they were saved from beyond a simple answer of "I was saved from my sin." While true, they don't understand, and many have never even heard, that before Christ they were enemies of God, separated from Him, hateful toward Him, and not seeking Him. Those without Christ don't exist in a state of neutrality where they are trying to choose Jesus or not. They exist in a state of sin where they are enslaved and defined by it.

I remember being approached by a youth worker at a church after preaching on this very topic. Her statement to me was that they had to do a lot of "damage control" because the topic was so heavy. She told me that her students had "never heard anything like that before, and it really affected them." I explained to her that is the exact reason why I chose to preach on the topic. We rob students of the joy of their salvation when they don't know what they've been saved from, and the reconciling work of Christ means much more when a student understands the depth of brokenness in the relationship that needed repair. The result is that students who begin to understand the depth of their salvation begin to fall more in love with Jesus because they see "behind the scenes" of what God really did for them.

Second, bring behavioral and lifestyle issues back to Jesus, always. This may sound simple, but the easy thing to do as a student pastor is to grab a verse and tell them what to do. The difficult, and better, thing to do is to draw it back to Jesus and the gospel. Let's take the issue of purity as an example. Here are some common ways that this issue is handled in student ministry: focus students on verses about how a believer's body is a temple; instruct them that sex should be saved until marriage; tell them the physiological dangers that exist for sexually active people; or guilt them into obedience by talking about how God isn't honored with their sexual immorality. In principle, I would agree with all of these things.

However, when an issue is handled in this way it places the focus on the student and the sin rather than Jesus and the righteousness He has already earned for your students. Here are some ways to handle this same issue while keeping Jesus at the center: focus students toward their identity as a believer and that God has declared them pure through Christ; help them to see that Jesus' death on the cross not only forgives them of sexual immorality but also empowers them to live a life of purity; teach them that God's grace is sufficient for them when mistakes are made and Jesus' sacrifice takes away their sin and the guilt; help them to realize that the Christian life isn't about trying harder but about dying to self and Jesus living through them.

This is a process that can be used with any issue, but it is difficult because it takes more time in preparation and more time for these truths to sink deeply into the hearts of your students. You will have to frequently connect the dots for them. Until your students know that you are going to connect it with Jesus before you say it, you haven't done it enough. When they expect it, they will begin to piece it together on their own even when you're not there.

Third, help them to see their identity through the grace of God rather than their personal failures. Help them to see that God's power is with them and He has equipped them to live out what He has commanded them to do. Constantly point them to the truth that through Christ they have been declared holy before God. It is finished. Then lead them to live in light of that declaration.

Student ministry isn't meant to be a conveyer belt that attempts to produce students who all look the same and act the same. Your students are all different, and their paths of discipleship will be different. Healthy student ministries are *Character Transforming* ministries whose goal is to help students stare at Jesus, allowing Him to transform their hearts and inform their decisions. The result is a group of students who are reproducing disciples of Jesus that view their lives as tools for God's glory.

Discussion Questions

1. How is our ministry similar to or different from the conveyor belt mentality?

2. What are some of the main behavioral issues that come up in our student ministry? When we teach about those issues, do we effectively focus the conversation back to Jesus?

3. Would our students say the Christian life is about trying harder, or would they say that it is about dying to self and Jesus living through them?

Chapter 7

Character Transformation and the Word

IN JOHN 15:5 JESUS SAYS, "I AM THE VINE; YOU ARE THE BRANCHES. THE one who remains in Me and I in him produces much fruit, because you can do nothing without Me." Jesus' words here are clear: unless your students remain in Him they will never produce the fruit of a disciple. Being connected to Jesus is the key component in developing students who are reproducing disciples who view their lives as tools for God's glory. Transformation cannot happen apart from Him, and the primary way that your students "remain" in Jesus is to "remain" in His Word.

Character Transforming ministries consistently point students to God's Word and help them apply those truths to the deepest parts of who they are. Student ministries can be known for a lot of things, and at this point in our culture we need more student ministries that are known for their faithful preaching of God's Word and an intense commitment to teach students how to study the Bible for themselves. Sadly, there are far too many students leaving for college with the Bible still feeling awkward in their hands.

George Guthrie, a professor at Union University, has documented his experience with biblical illiteracy firsthand. For several years he has given an eighteen-question, multiple-choice quiz to students in some of their first-year survey classes.

Questions include:

- How many temptations did Jesus experience in the wilderness?
- Which book is from the New Testament?

- Who was the person Pontius Pilate released during Jesus' trial?

He explains it this way on his website: "In the past three years the average score has been a 57 on the quiz! Their performance on this quiz is not abnormal for students across the country at top Christian universities. Similar quizzes at Wheaton and Seattle Pacific have similar results."[4]

Obviously, being able to answer Bible trivia isn't the goal of a student ministry, but this short survey reveals the tip of the iceberg for a problem that has been developing in student ministry for quite some time.

Student ministry in large part has been content to spoon-feed Scripture and application of that Scripture to students rather than teach them how to study the Bible for themselves. In an effort to help students understand the Bible and see that it can apply to life today, we have turned it into a roadmap for their lives. When the Bible becomes just a roadmap, or a list of rules, it becomes dull and boring. Students begin to see it as just one of the many textbooks or opinions that float in and out of their lives. When the Bible is taught this way either from the stage or in a small-group environment, the focus of the ministry centers on formation rather than transformation. Students begin to think that if the Bible is a roadmap for my life, then all I need to do is follow that roadmap.

At this point some of you may be thinking, "Yes, that is exactly what we want," but you don't want that because it doesn't last. Seeing the Bible in this way is no different than any other religious text that could be considered a "roadmap" for life in that religion. The Bible is unique because it allows a person to know Jesus—not just know about Him or a list of rules that He left behind, but to actually know Him.

Take a look at 2 Corinthians 3:18: "We all, with unveiled faces, are looking as in a mirror at the glory of the Lord and are being transformed into the same image from glory to glory; this is from the Lord who is the Spirit." Here, Paul tells us how transformation happens: a believer stares at the glory of the Lord and is then transformed into that image. Your students are going to be transformed into the image that they stare at most, and they're going to stare at something. There are plenty of things in our culture for them to stare at, and when we teach the Bible as a roadmap for their lives, it has the potential of leading them to stare in failure at the imperfection of their character rather than at the image of Jesus and His glory. Student ministry fails when it becomes about shaping a student's character apart from the life-giving power and freedom of the gospel found by knowing Jesus through His Word.

Teaching Scripture has taken a backseat to illustration and entertainment. Issues of relevancy and attention span have caused student ministries to dumb down the preaching and teaching of the Word to the point of minimal effectiveness. Personal creativity, devotional "talks," and haphazard disciple-ship plans have replaced preaching and strategic discipleship plans that lead people to learn how to study the Bible on their own. According to Christian Smith and the National Study of Youth and Religion, 32 percent of Protestant teenagers report reading the Bible alone at least once per week. While this stat is low and concerning, it doesn't even get into how many of them have a meaningful time with Jesus through His Word.

I'm all for creativity, excellence, and considering the audience when preparing a message, but those things aren't transforming the character of our students. In most cases, what we're left with is a student who graduates from an excellently run student ministry where they remember the awesome events and hilarious stories while the Bible still feels awkward in their hands. The solution?

Student pastors. Spend more time studying the Scripture and preparing to lead your students to God's Word than you do preparing your illustrations and games. What you will find is that many times Scripture is an excellent illustrator of Scripture. If your answer is "I don't have that kind of time," then you need to recruit some additional volunteers to help you with the less important so you can focus on what matters.

Develop a strategic discipleship plan that has a clear scope and sequence that leads students to stare at Jesus through His Word. As a side note, "We study God's Word" is not a plan. It may sound really spiritual, but randomly deciding what passages you will study each week or telling your leaders to choose the passages they want to study based on their group is not a plan. If developing a plan yourself sounds too daunting, and it is for many, then partner with a trusted curriculum provider that has done that work for you. It isn't a cop-out to do this; it's smart because it gets you a lot of time back to do ministry.

Finally, train your leaders on how to lead a group of students and how to teach the Bible well. There are three main ways I would suggest to accomplish this training. First, practice on each other. Have groups of leaders talk through issues that may come up and how they will handle them. Second, teach through the curriculum as an example to your leaders on how you want them to lead. Model it for them during one, or many, of your training meetings. Third, invite experts to lead training at your church. These experts can be people within your church or even your student ministry that do a tremendous job, as well as someone outside of your church that can give your leaders a different perspective. I've often found this outside perspective can be extremely valuable as you train your volunteer leaders.

Volunteer leaders. Approach your small group with the mind-set that you are going to teach your students how to study the Bible. Avoid giving them all the answers and reading every passage for them. Make them get in their Bibles.

Develop a plan for your group to memorize Scripture together as you work through your curriculum. Prepare for each session. Group leaders who prepare haphazardly will lead the same way. Follow the plan that your student pastor has laid out for you. There's a reason the plan has been given, and "going rogue" with your group will begin to break down the discipleship plan and eventually break down unity in the ministry as a whole.

Discussion Questions

1. How would you rate the biblical literacy of our student ministry?

2. How often do we spend time in God's Word as student ministry leaders?

3. How can we begin to teach from the stage and lead in small groups in order to equip students to study the Bible on their own?

Chapter 8

Character Transformation and Theology

AS A STUDENT MINISTRY LEADER, YOU SEE STUDENTS COME AND GO all the time. One minute a student seems to be living for the Lord, and the next minute they seem to have lost all interest. It wouldn't take you very long to come up with the name of a student who seemed to be on the right track when they were young but began to struggle spiritually as they entered high school or left for college. Some of those names are still in my mind years later. Let me suggest a possible solution to this problem.

No, this isn't an all-sufficient miracle cure, but to call it just one piece of the puzzle would be to understate it. Instead, it should be seen as the most important section of any puzzle: the frame. More than likely, one of the first things you learned about putting a puzzle together was to start with the frame. This is because it provides a starting point as well as the support for the finished work. When your ministry is a *Character Transforming* ministry, the finished puzzle is a student who is a reproducing disciple of Jesus who views their life as a tool for God's glory.

Equipping your students theologically helps them see the pieces of their life through the right frame: God. We have to help them see the magnitude of who God is and allow Him to be the one that guides them through the rest of the pieces of their lives.

Students in your ministry have many different frames for their lives: success, religion, good behavior, spiritual checklists, athletics, etc. As you know, each one of these frames will only lead them to spiritual failure. Students need to see that the right frame is God Himself—that God is worth worshipping, worth the glory they are to give, and worth their entire lives.

If puzzles aren't your thing, think about it this way: equipping your students theologically builds the skeletal structure that the outward flesh of the Christian life can hang on. Without your skeletal structure, you would be a pile of unmoving flesh. Your flesh can't stand on its own. Spiritually, your students are the same. When we focus only on the outward flesh of the Christian life but never help them build the skeletal structure, they will be left lying in a heap on the ground the first time they have to make a decision without you or their parent present to give them the right answer.

As students begin to build a skeleton of theology and doctrine, it will provide the support they need to filter through the many decisions of life in a God-honoring way. As a student pastor you want students in your ministry to share the gospel, make disciples, and live a holy life. Some common ways to motivate students to do that are to constantly talk about it, guilt them into it, or explain the benefits of living that way. These are temporary approaches that result in short-term impact. The *Character Transforming* ministry will engage students in the challenging things of their faith and lead them to understand the "why" behind what they believe. In a *Character Transforming* ministry, students will be challenged with the intellectual side of their faith as well as the behavioral side of their faith. As your students see more of who God is and how He interacts with them, they develop an intense love for Him that can't help but affect their lifestyles.

Equipping students theologically, if done correctly, will always lead them to God's Word. Students will begin to understand the way they know God is through His Word. As they know God more, their view of Him grows and their love for Him grows, as does their love for His Word. Wayne Grudem writes in his systematic theology book, "The more we know about God, His Word, and His relationships to the world and mankind, the better we will trust Him, the more fully we will praise Him, and the more readily we will obey Him."[5] Many times the discipling process of a student begins with the flesh, the worship and obedience part, without giving any attention to the bone structure that supports that flesh.

Correct study of theology and doctrine won't lead to a knowledge that puffs up (1 Cor. 8:1), but rather a life that loves, worships, and obeys God.

As a middle school and high school student I was never exposed to the intellectual side of my faith. I never heard words like sanctification, propitiation, and justification. It wasn't until I was a middle school pastor (five years after graduating from high school and pre-seminary) serving at a church in Alabama that I was challenged to think through what I really believed about the Trinity, election, the atonement, the relationship between God's sovereignty and evil in the world, and a whole host of other theological issues. I was never confronted with why the virgin birth was so important to what I believed. I knew it was, but the "why" was missing. It wasn't until I was challenged with these things that my view of God began to expand far beyond the borders of my mind.

A former pastor of mine, Buddy Gray, always said, "The most important thing about you is your view of God." I came face-to-face with that reality serving on his staff in Alabama. As my view of God expanded, so did my love for Him and my desire to worship Him. Out of that personal experience with God, I vowed to make sure that students in my ministries would always be challenged theologically. This happened at various levels. First, it changed the way I prepared to preach and the content I was preaching. Theological concepts became a part of my preaching and teaching at an entry level in nearly every message. I wanted to make sure that all my students heard and were familiar with sanctification, propitiation, justification, their meanings, and the results in their lives. Some of the major doctrines of our faith: the inerrancy of Scripture, the Trinity, the incarnation of Jesus, and an understanding of the Five Solas also fit into this category of entry level familiarity for my students.

We also began to have students in our home once a week to read through and discuss systematic theology books chapter by chapter, as well as other books that would challenge us theologically and doctrinally. These reading groups were something that I continued to do for the next decade, and they became one of the most impactful components of my ministry in every church I served. To this day I have students and families thank me for this aspect of the ministries I've had the privilege to lead, and in each case they talk about the impact it has made on their lives over the years. Do they remember everything? No, but their view of God is expanded, and they began to realize that they serve a big God. When students realize that they are serving a big God, they begin to understand that this big God can do and has done big things with them. It increases their worship, their obedience, and their love for Him and others.

Here's what I learned: students can handle a lot more than we give them credit for, and leading a ministry this way will be a constant challenge for you and your leaders. You will be challenged to continue learning personally, which is a good thing. Your preparation to preach and teach will be challenged because you will need to present theological concepts in a way that your students can grasp. There is a ramping up process with your students in this area, and your teaching should ease them into theological concepts at a macro level. You will also be challenged with vision casting and communication to your volunteer teams to help them see how equipping students theologically is essential in a student's character transformation process.

Character transformation and theology are linked together because theology, when taught correctly, will help a person know God. As a student in your ministry begins to know God, the result will be a greater love for God. This greater love for God will result in a growing desire to obey God and live a life of dependence upon Him. At the end of this process is actual character transformation that lasts rather than a short-term adjustment to their behavior.

Another result of this process is that your students will begin to enjoy the Lord. They will delight in Him, in worshipping Him, and in spending time with Him. Church will become something they want to be part of, not because it is awesome or fun or social (these things aren't bad), but because they want to be with other believers to express their faith together. Joy is missing in the culture of our students today. They don't have it and don't know how to find it. I've seen this to be true in student ministries that I've led personally and in ones that I see through speaking. Even ones who are seen as leaders or strong believers in the ministry struggle with finding real joy in the Lord. The antidote for this problem is blowing a student's mind with who God is. Teach them theology for their own good.

Help them see the end result of this process, and realize that not everyone will be on board at first. As a volunteer leader you will be challenged to continue growing as well, again a good thing. Don't be content to rest on the spiritual knowledge that you've always had. There is so much more of God out there for you to discover and enjoy as well. Allow your own view of God to expand as you seek to help a student's view do the same. There may be times when you are fearful of teaching something you aren't completely familiar with or not being able to answer a student's question. The students in your group aren't looking for you to have all the answers. They're looking for you to be able to discuss with them and guide them to the places where they can find the answers. Be willing to go on this theological journey together.

Your students need a backbone. The reality is that they're going to construct one. It will either be God or something of their own creation. Student ministries have a great responsibility to help them build a backbone that will last, a frame that will allow them to assemble the rest of their lives in a way that honors God. Equip your students theologically, not to fill their heads with knowledge, but to construct a godly backbone that results in a student who is a reproducing disciple of Jesus and a tool for God's glory.

Discussion Questions

1. How would you rate our ministry's effectiveness in the area of theological discipleship?

2. What are some of the frames that our students attempt to build their lives around? How can we help them build their lives around the correct frame?

3. Are there some things we need to change organizationally to make more room/time for theological discipleship in our ministry?

Chapter 9

Character Transformation and Grace

I LED WORSHIP ONE TIME AS A STUDENT PASTOR. IT WAS AT MY FIRST church in Huntsville, Alabama, and our normal worship leader wasn't able to make it to the service. Four months prior to this night, I started learning to play the guitar. Knowing I was going to serve as a student pastor, hopefully soon, I thought knowing how to play the guitar would be a great skill and one that would come in handy at some point. This "some point" became that night for a room full of students. It was the first time I'd ever played in front of anyone, and I picked the three easiest songs I had been practicing that I thought I could nail.

Practice and sound check went better than I thought they would, and I was ready to go. Then the students came in. Everything fell apart for me as nervousness took over. My confident sound check turned into a train wreck from the beginning as I forgot to make sure my guitar was in tune before I began. Through the three-song set I battled through nervousness, extreme sweat, wrong words, and an out-of-tune guitar to deliver the worst worship leading experience of all time. The only comment made to my face about that night was the ever-encouraging, "That really took a lot of courage, doing what you did tonight," from an adult volunteer. I never led worship again.

At this point in my life I can look back at that moment and laugh, but what I didn't realize then is that I never had a chance because my guitar was out of tune. When a musical instrument is out of tune, you can try your hardest to make it sound good, but it won't work. The only thing you can do to make it sound good once again is to stop what you're doing and tune it. As bad as an instrument can sound when it is out of tune, when in tune a musical instrument or group of instruments can make some of the most beautiful sounds we could ever hear, and in that moment the instrument is fulfilling its purpose.

Grace works the same way as a musical instrument. It's something we have to be tuned for in order to understand it and live by it. There's a line in the hymn "Come Thy Fount of Every Blessing," that says, "Tune my heart to sing Thy grace." The reason this plea is included in the hymn is because people aren't naturally tuned to grace. The hymn also says, "We are prone to wander." Most often when we think of this "wandering" we think in terms of sinfulness. However, we are also prone to wander into rule following, self-righteousness, laziness, and an identity defined by our own ability. Those all happen to be areas of sinfulness as well; we just tend to ignore them more often than other sins because they are well camouflaged in spiritual language or intentions.

Our "natural tuning" is toward these things, and the result is the kind of life that experiences grace at salvation but defines the disciple's life in terms of a spiritual checklist, self-righteousness, and human effort. Grace is the opposite of these things. Grace is the unmerited favor of God. Grace is getting something that you don't deserve. Grace is the power to live each day fighting temptation and the power to get back up when we fall. Grace is what binds our wandering heart to Him. Grace is what fuels our moment-by-moment dependence on God to live the life He's called us to live. That's what it means for our hearts to sing the grace of God and for you to lead a *Character Transforming* student ministry—your heart must be tuned to sing God's grace.

When your heart isn't tuned toward grace, not only will it affect your personal discipleship, it will also bend your teaching to be predominantly focused on discipleship through checklists, serving Christ out of a self-righteous willpower, and the consequences of sin. Each one of these areas, when not filtered by the grace of God, will lead students to failure rather than transformation.

There are two common misunderstandings that exist when we talk about a more grace-driven approach to teaching students. The first is that it will lead them into more sin rather than teaching them the way they need to live. This is not a new thought. In fact, it's the same misunderstanding Paul is addressing in Romans 6:1 when he asks the question, "Should we continue in sin so that grace may multiply?" The answer is obviously no, but the reason he gives is significant. He doesn't point the people back to a spiritual checklist or human effort in their spiritual transformation. Rather, Paul argues that a person truly living by grace will become more like Christ rather than go on sinning because they've died with Christ, now live with Him (in His strength and power), and have freedom from sin's enslavement.

The second misunderstanding is that a grace-driven approach to teaching is too abstract a concept and students need something concrete that they can readily grasp and assimilate into their lives right now. As teachers, it's our duty to move what may seem like an abstract concept toward the concrete so that our learners can understand. It's also our duty to help them learn how to move from abstract to concrete on their own. We do them no favors if we give them all the answers all the time. It's okay for your students to think and it is okay for them to be stretched mentally with the things of God. Put the "carrot" out in front of them just enough for them to reach and chase after the answers themselves.

In some sense, that is your role as a student leader. You are meant to lead them to a destination, not carry them on your back while you go to a destination. Here's what this looks like at a practical level for you as a leader of students. A Christian student knows what it's like to fail in their sin. They don't need to be taught what that looks like. As a response to this, because of their concrete thinking, they believe they are supposed to live a life of victory over sin. Then they hear teaching that focuses on a spiritual checklist, and they connect the dots concluding that victory over sin comes from fulfilling a list. They think, "If I can just accomplish this list then I will have victory over what is causing me to fail time and time again."

This is not grace-driven teaching, and it won't lead to transformation in their lives. Grace-driven teaching would show the student that they don't need to live a life of victory over sin because the victory has already been won for them. It would show them that yes, the standard placed against them is perfection; but that perfection was earned for them through the life of Christ, and because of His sacrifice they are already perfect. Jerry Bridges, in his book *Pursuit of Holiness,* gives us a great perspective on this topic. He states that God doesn't want our victory, He wants our obedience.

This is crucial for a student's transformational process because until they realize the victory has already been won, they will just keep trying to throw themselves at the wall of human effort until they feel victorious. The beauty in teaching students to understand grace comes when they begin to realize that they don't have to sin any longer because Jesus has broken "sin's dominion over the body" (Rom. 6:6). Jesus earned victory for them, and through Him they have the power to walk in obedience. If you're going to lead a ministry focused on transformation, then your teaching needs to be dripping with that truth.

Learning to teach grace is a continual process. The same is true for me. It isn't something that will happen overnight because our hearts aren't naturally tuned that way. It's something that needs to be thought through and wrestled with personally before it comes out effectively to students. If you choose to teach this way, there will be those who disagree. What you are teaching will sound out of tune to them, but stay the course. You aren't in your role to make everyone happy. You are there to, with grace and respect, lead a ministry that sees the lives of students transformed. In spending a lot of time with students and teaching this way for years, I've continually seen three themes of grace rise to the surface as most important in a student's transformation. They are: living in grace each day, experiencing true forgiveness, and extending grace to others.

Students struggle to live in the power of grace each day for the same reason we do: it's easy to slip out of tune and begin to focus once again on self-righteousness and human effort. Crucial to them understanding how to live in the power of grace each day is the truth that Paul presents in both

Colossians 3:3 and Galatians 2:20: the idea that they have died and the life they now live is one that is "hidden with Christ" (Colossians) and "Christ lives in me" (Galatians). Both of these passages reveal the reality that this life is not their life. They died to the old self, and their new life is wrapped up and consumed in Jesus.

For students, this is the issue of dependence. They live each day trying to find something to depend on that will give them identity, love, hope, and significance. God's design is that His people have a moment-by-moment dependence upon Him, that He is where their identity, love, hope, and significance are found. It is His amazing grace that motivates and strengthens His people to live His way. As you lead students to God's Word, where they will continually come into contact with His grace, it will strengthen their moment-by-moment dependence on Him resulting in the lifestyle changes that many student ministries seek first.

Few students continually live in the forgiveness of God that is total and complete. Throughout my years as a student pastor, the theme of forgiveness was a constant one as students would talk with me about their struggles. They couldn't understand why they couldn't move past their issues, and it was heartbreaking to see the pain on their face as their desire for the Lord was held back by some sin.

One student stands out in particular for me. He, unfortunately like many guys in our culture, was struggling deeply with pornography and masturbation. As he fought this addiction it became clear that he was fighting it from a place of human effort and willpower. This was a student who knew the passages I mentioned in the last section. He knew his life wasn't his, that Jesus had freed him from that sin, that he could fight in Jesus' power and not his own, yet he still fell out of tune and failed in his own willpower. So what was missing? His understanding of forgiveness. He knew that he was forgiven and that his future was forgiven, but he was so overcome by the guilt of his past sin that he was paralyzed. His guilt kept him from experiencing a grace-filled life each day.

Forgiveness is difficult for students to grasp immediately because people don't forgive that way. God is the only one who forgives totally and completely, so there's no reference point for them. The only way to remedy this is to once again take them to Scripture, lifting out the themes of forgiveness at every turn.

There are too many student ministries that focus their students toward the consequences of sin as a motivator. Yes, sin has consequences, the first and foremost being a direct offense to a holy God, which ironically rarely makes the cut when people teach on the consequences of sin. In those moments with my student I could have easily kept hammering the consequences of his sin, but what he needed to understand most was the total and complete forgiveness of God.

Colossians 3 continues to give us insight here. My student, and yours, need to understand that to be hidden with Christ means both He lives through him in the future, but also lived for him in the past. God no longer sees his sin or his guilt. Jesus' life became his life, and the abolishment of sin included the abolishment of the associated guilt. This view doesn't rob God of His justice or His view of sin. It shows the beauty of both His justice and forgiveness at the cross. It is from that place of understanding forgiveness that a student can move on to Colossians 3:5 and begin to put to death what belonged to their worldly nature. Guilt brings shame. Grace brings freedom. Lead your students to freedom.

This will surprise you: students can be mean. They can be rude, insensitive, exclusive, and gossipy. At moments even the ones you would say are leaders in your ministry can have flashes of this kind of behavior.

Do you want to know if your students are growing in grace? Look at how they are showing grace to other people. A person who is truly learning to live in God's grace each day will begin to show that same grace to the people around them in a growing manner. Grace can't help but spill out of a person's life who is living by it. They will be a person of forgiveness because they know what it is like to be forgiven. They will be a person of God's Word because it is only through being connected to the Vine that we really understand what grace is, and they will be a person who leads others to be connected to the Vine. They will be a person of worship as their hearts are continually tuned to sing the beautiful notes of God's grace.

This is where teaching grace gets difficult. If you as a leader are going to teach grace effectively, then you too must be a person who lives in grace, experiences true forgiveness, and extends grace to others. As with evangelism, your students won't truly become people of grace unless they see their leadership modeling this behavior. As leaders it's easy for us to slip into a mode where we rely on our own strength to make ministry happen. You know how to do ministry, the plans that need to be made and the forms that need to be filled out. It can be easy to forget God in all of that, but modeling a grace-filled life to your students will show them how you rely on God's strength and power each day.

At some point, and probably at multiple points throughout your ministry, you will fight the temptation to find your identity in things other than Christ. For student ministry leaders, oftentimes we want to be the ones who ride in and save the day for a student, and if we aren't careful that can begin to be where our identity is found. Forgiveness is difficult. The idea is easy, but the application for us as leaders can be just as much of a struggle as it is for our students. Personally, I've struggled with guilt, and it is a constant discipline when that struggle arises to go to God and rest in His forgiveness instead of being swallowed by the Enemy's guilt tactics.

Then there's the whole "showing grace to others" part. How do you handle disagreements when they come up? How do you show grace to your family and friends? Students notice all of these things, and they are taking cues from you. Ultimately, your motivation to live a grace-filled life shouldn't be because of your students. If it is, you will fail. However, the fact remains that if we are going to teach grace, then the best teacher is how our lives match up with what we say from the stage or in the small group.

Discussion Questions

1. How can helping your students understand the perfect life of Christ help them live for Him right now?

2. How can we as leaders model what it looks like to live a life of dependence upon God?

3. What needs to happen in our own lives for us to be more in tune with grace?

Chapter 10

Character Transformation and Small Groups

"RED ROVER, RED ROVER, SEND BILLY RIGHT OVER." THIS IS A PHRASE that for many of you will bring a flood of memories to your brain. Even now you are picturing the kid, maybe it was you, who was repeatedly clotheslined as he or she tried to break the chain of arms at the other end of the field. Red Rover is one of those classic schoolyard games. Sadly, it is also a game that has decreased in popularity due to fear of concussion and the self-esteem degradation of being picked as the weakest person in the line to be "sent over." Ah, what a great game.

As with any game, over time strategies are developed to help you win. For Red Rover, teams began to learn that the way to keep an opposing team member from breaking through the line, regardless of their size and strength, was to have elasticity to your line. You don't win Red Rover by trying to grip each other's wrists and hands as tight as you can. You win when the entire line collapses at the point of attack and bends with the two people who have been picked out as the target. Red Rover at its core is a game about community and not about having the strongest person on your team.

We can learn a lot from this game and from the strategy that it takes to win. In order for your students to experience transformation, they need to be connected to a small group (Sunday school, life group, home group, etc.). Yes, transformation can happen in a number of environments, and I'm not suggesting that small groups are the only way. However, I am suggesting that small groups are the best way. Here's why.

Your small groups place students in community together and give them an opportunity to link arms with each other and live out the partnership in the gospel that they are meant to have (Phil. 1:3–6). This partnership in the gospel that students experience through being part of a small group is a vehicle that Jesus will use to carry to completion the work that He began in them. Because of this, your small-group ministry is essential to their transformation. Your students experience hardship on a regular basis. They will struggle, will have moments of drama come in and out of their lives, and will be attacked by the Enemy as they pursue Jesus. The group of students that they experience life with, that they link arms with, the ones that they partner together in the gospel with, will be the ones who bend and collapse around them when they experience these struggles. They are the people the Lord will use to make sure the line doesn't break with the force of the attack.

Sadly, many student ministries put little to no emphasis on their small groups. All of the creative and strategic energy is poured into a Wednesday night service or event and the small-group ministry is seen as something that just has to be done because the rest of the church does it. When your small-group ministry gets the leftovers of your time and energy, it cripples the transformation that takes place in your ministry. Here are some of the problems that will exist in a ministry that has a lack of focus on small groups:

1. Students that are saved and baptized in your church will become stagnant in their growth.

2. There will be a lack of unity in the ministry as a whole.

3. Students will struggle to build lasting, spiritually focused relationships.

4. Students will become fatigued of a ministry that is all hype and focused on nothing more than "bring your friends next week."

5. It will be difficult for you to recruit and keep quality volunteers who want to invest in students.

6. There will be few students who have mentoring type relationships with volunteer leaders, which results in a ministry's inability to minister to students at a deeper level at the times they need it most.

7. Students will fall through the cracks and drop out of the ministry without anyone noticing their absence.

There isn't a student pastor or volunteer leader in existence who would willingly sign up to have any one of these problems or who would describe this kind of ministry as healthy. You might even be thinking, "Wow, that sounds a little extreme." You're right. It is extreme. It's extremely common in student ministries across the country and is a contributing factor in the overall discipleship vacuum that we are seeing in student ministry today. If your small groups have been getting the leftovers of your ministry there's still hope. Stop neglecting the transformational engine of your ministry. There are many things you can do to create the kind of small groups that bring about transformation and help students live in partnership in the gospel. I want to focus you toward the three most important.

First, recruit leaders that share this vision for small groups. You can't do it all by yourself. In fact, if you are trying to do ministry on your own, you aren't doing it biblically. Ephesians 4:11–12 is clear when Paul states that the role of a pastor is to train the saints in the work of the ministry. Not only is it biblical, it's just smart. Your ministry will see more disciples made as you multiply yourself than if you were to attempt to do it all on your own. You need people of like mind to join you in your task of making disciples of students and their families, but not just any person will do. You need to recruit people who share your same vision for student ministry, specifically the purpose of your small groups. For that to happen, you need a vision and you need to be able to clearly articulate that vision during your recruitment meetings.

As the student pastor it's your responsibility to make sure your vision is understood before a leader takes on any kind of ongoing volunteer role. True leaders reproduce who they are, and when you place a leader in charge of a small group, you want to make sure that what they are reproducing fits with the direction that God has given you for the ministry. Your recruitment process should also be a long one. Having an empty chair is better than having the wrong person fill a chair.

Doug Fields, in his book *Your First Two Years in Youth Ministry,* talks about having high barriers to entry to serve in your ministry and low barriers to quit serving in your ministry.

Those are wise words, and the times when I haven't followed that advice in my own leader recruitment I have paid the price. Before you bring someone into a key role in the transformational process of the students God has placed in your ministry, you need to know them, their salvation story, what God has taught them recently, what their daily time with Him is like, if they are passionate about students, and the list could go on forever. The bottom line is this: passing a background check and breathing shouldn't be the only qualifications for someone to serve in your ministry.

If you are a volunteer reading this, I want you to know how important it is that you follow the leadership of the student pastor at your church. When you joined up as a student ministry volunteer, you placed yourself under his or her authority in that specific ministry. Join in the vision for ministry and for small groups that has been communicated to you. A leader doing their own thing in the midst of the student ministry is never healthy, and it always leads to disunity. If you have a disagreement, it is your responsibility to go to your student pastor and have a grace-filled and clear conversation about what you're thinking. If you continue to have a disagreement about the direction of the ministry, barring some type of moral failure or gross neglect, then it is your responsibility to walk away from the ministry rather than become a cancer that eats away at the culture and unity of the ministry from the inside.

Second, train your leaders. Recruiting someone to join you in ministry isn't the final step in this process. It's the first step. Again, Ephesians 4:12 implies that pastors will seek out other people to join them in ministry, but it doesn't stop there. It also clearly states that these people should be trained to do the work. When your recruiting process is finished, it won't work to just throw a leader into a group and walk away. Take the time to develop a plan to develop them in their leadership of students. They are looking for this from you and desperately want help to become a better leader. When you develop your plan, make sure you are six months to a year ahead of schedule. Your training plan should include ministry-wide meetings, fellowship opportunities, and constant relational connections so that you have the pulse of what's going on in the ministry.

These leaders will be able to give you great insight into the students, and their feedback should never be discounted.

As you train you will need to recast vision continually. You know you've cast the vision enough when your leaders are repeating the vision to you and you begin to hear students using the language of the vision that they heard from their leaders. Until it seeps that far into the culture of the ministry, you need to continue the vision work. The biggest thing to remember about training your leaders is that it is a form of discipleship. As you develop them, they will develop students. For many of you, I know that this training component isn't high on your list of priorities or maybe even in your gift mix, but it is worth it. It's worth it because you can't possibly know each student in your ministry at a deep enough level to know when they are struggling. Even if you do, you can't minister effectively to each of these students at the same time. This is where your leaders come in. Through the small-group environment, your leaders will be able to have meaningful relationships where they can notice when a student is struggling. Your leaders will be able to minister to those students in a way that you can't because of that relationship. This isn't abandonment on your part. It's good discipleship. Your students need relationships with adult volunteers who will speak the truth of God's Word into their lives at the moments when they need it most. Healthy student ministries, ones that see the lives of students transformed, have a culture of leadership development.

Third, make God's Word central. There's no substitute or shortcut for binding students together in the gospel. The only way is a constant dose of the gospel itself, through His Word. The students in your small groups don't need your opinion or the opinion of another leader. They need the Scriptures. They need a place to discuss and process in community what God is teaching them. They need a safe place to question and wrestle with theological concepts. They need a place where they can talk about their struggles. They need a place where they can confess their sin and seek accountability. All of these things should take place in your groups, but they become dangerous if there isn't an umbrella of God's Word over it all. A great small-group leader will lead students to Scripture at every turn. As students experience all of these things and are led to

Scripture for their answers, a love for God's Word will begin to develop within them. For students in my own ministry, many times their love of God's Word began in a small-group environment and moved to their personal devotional life where it began to flourish.

Your small groups are important, too important to give them your leftovers. They are where your students are most likely to experience transformation. They are where your students will learn how to partner in the gospel together. They are where your students will begin to disciple each other, and that is a truly beautiful thing.

Discussion Questions

1. As it stands now, is your small group ministry getting your best work or your leftovers?

2. What is the vision for your small-group ministry? Is it known by the other leaders and the students?

3. What can we do to get more students connected to a small group? What needs to happen for our students to experience community within their small group?

Culture Shaping

Chapter 11

Element #3: Culture Shaping

TAKE A MOMENT AND THINK ABOUT THE STUDENTS IN YOUR MINISTRY. Now focus in on the most squirrelly, off-the-wall student you have. I know exactly which student it would be for me. In thirteen years of student ministry and three different churches, one student rises above all the others in this category. He was the kid who as a sixth grader jumped on my back every time he saw me. He stole my hat every time I wore one. He tried to eat his weight in pizza at every event, and his small-group leaders continually asked how they could get him to calm down and listen. Sound familiar?

One of those students exists in every ministry. With that student pictured in your mind, I want to ask you a question. Do you believe your students can shape the culture in which they live? Do you believe that student, the one who changes your phone language to Portuguese, can truly shape the culture?

Keep that question in your mind for just a moment. A simple definition for culture that we can work with here is "a set of beliefs, values, and way of life for a group of people." This generation of students has a culture that is different from yours. They think and believe differently than you do now and differently from when you were a teenager. Your students' culture will have slight, sometimes significant, differences from other student cultures depending on the environment and context in which you minister. You've seen evidence of this clearly even in your own town.

For example, think about the high school or high schools in your area. Chances are there will be several cultures that exist even within one school or from school to school. It's important to note that while culture is often used to describe race or ethnicity, and culture is definitely involved in that conversation, race and ethnicity are not the only driving factors for culture. There's nothing wrong with cultural differences, but it is a reminder that ministry context matters. What works for you in your context programmatically may not work in another area of the country in the same way. It may also be true that one ministry endeavor that you do in your town will reach a certain group of people while another group of people may not be interested at all. It's important to get to know the culture and even subcultures of the area in which you serve.

So, if culture is a set of beliefs, values, and a way of life for a group of people, then developing culture-shaping students will mean your students shape the beliefs, values, and way of life for the people around them. It means they will make an impact in the places God has placed them. Back to our original question: Do you believe the students in your ministry can shape the culture in which they live?

Your answer to this question will determine a great deal about how you lead as a student pastor or volunteer leader. For many, students are considered too young or immature to make a *Culture Shaping* difference in the world. Sure, they can make a difference with some friends, in their neighborhood, or even rarely on their school campus. But shaping the culture? Really? It is with that mind-set that student ministry degenerates into a holding tank while the adults are discipled or at best turns into years of "preparation" for them to get ready to do something big for the Lord.

The core of this thought is that students are weak. That may be true. In many ways they are weak and immature. They are in the most awkward season of development they will ever experience, and they have little in the way of resources. Yet God, who is all-powerful and can do whatever He pleases, has chosen to use the weak things of the world to exert His influence (Ps. 8:1–2; 1 Cor. 1:26–29). This is a message students rarely hear, and because of that they don't believe they can have *Culture Shaping* influence. For the majority of students, the culture is seen as either an immovable force that moves them wherever it wills or it is something they never think about at all. Both beliefs are unacceptable for a follower of Jesus.

One of my greatest joys in ministry now is the opportunity I have to speak with a lot of student pastors and volunteer leaders at conferences and training seminars. Within the last year of the writing of this book, I was at a conference speaking to a group of student pastors about this very topic. One of the student pastors raised his hand to stop me and spoke emotionally about the importance of instilling the belief in students that they can shape their culture. He talked about how he grew up in a student ministry and this belief was never instilled in him. It wasn't that the ministry was bad. It was just that this type of student empowerment was never talked about. When he finished I asked the rest of the room how many of them grew up in a student ministry that instilled in them the belief that they could shape their culture, maybe not with that specific language, but the general idea of having impact that could reach the ends of the earth. There wasn't a single person.

Students don't grow up believing they can shape the culture in which they live. In student ministry we get so distracted by wanting students to stay out of trouble or live right or even read their Bibles and pray that we forget to tell them that God has called them to do great things for Him and that in His strength and power they can truly be a *Culture Shaping* influence in our world.

I've fallen prey to this very thing. For a period of time in my own student ministry leadership, I focused too much on trying to get students to behave like a "Christian" instead of teaching them how they could actually shape the culture around them. Here's what I missed and what I believe many student ministries miss today: student ministry isn't just about helping kids stand apart from the culture; it's also about training them to shape it. Yes, lifestyle and spiritual disciplines are involved in this development, but if you are going to have a truly healthy student ministry, you will lead students far beyond just looking different from the culture to actually engaging and making an impact in it. This principle hit home for me while I ministered to a group of students I love dearly to this day.

This group of students loved the Lord. They really were the ones you dream about as a student pastor. They were at everything we did, actually read their Bibles frequently, had active prayer lives, and talked about the things God was teaching them all the time. They made an effort to live differently from the culture around them. They frequently talked about their desire to live a lifestyle that was "set apart," and as I continued to disciple them I encouraged them in this pursuit. All of these things are positive, but as this group of students entered into the latter years of high school I began to see that they became so set apart that they weren't having any influence on the people around them. They had become so withdrawn from the culture that all they were learning and experiencing with Jesus became something that stayed within their little group rather than shaping the beliefs, values, and way of life of their classmates and others within the ministry. And I encouraged this to happen. I led them to this place, and it punched me in the gut years later. You're called to more than helping students live a life that is "set apart" from the culture. Students from your ministry must realize their role as a believer is to engage in and shape their culture.

We see biblical evidence of this in Matthew 5:13–16 when Jesus uses three pictures to illustrate a believer's role in the world. Jesus says that we are the salt of the earth, a city on a hill, and a light placed on a lampstand. All three of these pictures show us that our faith isn't meant to be lived personally and quietly in a closet. You can't hide salt's presence in something. A city wasn't placed on the top of a hill to be ignored or hidden, and Jesus tells us the lamp "gives light for all who are in the house." This is true regardless of personality type, awkwardness level, and giftedness. Jesus doesn't make an age clarification in this passage. The students in your ministry are meant to live a life of influence. To be a follower of Jesus is to be a *Culture Shaping* influence. The two cannot be separated; and as such it is time that student ministries begin proclaiming to students that God, who doesn't need anyone or anything, chooses to use those who are weak. He is attracted to childlike faith and dependence upon Him. As student pastors and leaders, you must believe and lead knowing the truth that students are not merely the church of the future who are in a holding tank of preparation but people who God will use to shape the culture around us right now. Challenge your students with this reality.

Discussion Questions

1. Do our students believe they can shape the culture in which they live?

2. How would you rate the current level of influence our students have in their world?

3. What can we do to help our students see and act on the truth of Matthew 5:13–16?

Chapter 12

Student Leadership

INSTILLING THE BELIEF IN STUDENTS THAT THEY CAN BE A *CULTURE Shaping* influence goes far beyond teaching and telling them. Though that is an important part, it just isn't enough on its own. This leads us to an important question for you as a student ministry leader: How can we help (and equip) students see their *Culture Shaping* potential?

One of the best ways you can unlock this potential within a student is to give them leadership opportunities within your ministry. This has been an area of passion of mine throughout my years in student ministry. In every church I've served I've made developing student leaders one of my top priorities. I want to warn you: developing student leaders isn't easy. It will take a lot of your time, but it is worth it. And, because you are recruiting and developing other adult leaders to serve with you in ministry, you should begin to have the time freed up to place more emphasis in this area. I can honestly say that along with theology and doctrine, which we read about earlier, developing student leaders has had a greater impact on the students in my ministry than anything else.

This can be a much simpler process than what you might be thinking right now. For me, student leadership began by inviting students to join teams that would help us accomplish tasks that any student ministry would already want to accomplish. We didn't brainstorm any new ideas or start any new programs in the beginning. Students who were interested in leadership signed up for a team they thought would fit their personalities and leadership desires.

The teams I used were outreach, greeter, prayer, inreach, and service. The primary roles of the outreach and inreach teams were to call and connect with people inside the church, as well as those who had visited recently. The service team was responsible for developing community missions opportunities, and the prayer team led a prayer time before each Wednesday night service and managed a prayer request box in our student area. I also had adult volunteer leaders assigned to each of these teams to help with the organization and teach the students how to lead in a team setting. The goal was to eventually hand these teams over to students entirely with adult leaders supervising from a distance. As the students learned and grew, the adults could step back. From there, students always began to come up with their own ideas for ministry and leadership. My goal was always to help them figure out how to accomplish their ideas in a setting where they could succeed; but if they failed, then help them learn and grow in their leadership. I, as well as my adult leaders, never did the tasks for them. Students don't learn leadership if you always do things for them. They need to get in the middle of it, have chances to fail, and get their hands dirty trying to lead and do ministry alongside you.

It is one of the greatest feelings in the world when a student begins to believe they can lead and influence. It changes their view of how God wants to use them and unlocks the door for them to begin understanding what it means to live their life like that city on a hill from Matthew 5. In fact, many of those leadership team students throughout the years are now serving in some missions or ministry role.

The first step in giving students leadership opportunities is to study your own ministry context, your own students, and make decisions from there about the best way to get them involved. Right now, there are various levels of leadership talent and readiness within your students. There isn't a one-size-fits-all model. Not every student is ready to be given the highest level of leadership and responsibility within your ministry while others will show more potential early on. The goal here is to take a student from "point A" in their leadership involvement to "point B," wherever those points are now.

Remember that each student is different and needs to be discipled differently, which is where your adult volunteers come in yet again. It's important to realize that not every student will want to engage in leadership. Personality type and level of shyness are all contributing factors in a student's decision to take on some kind of leadership role, but that doesn't mean you should let them stay where they are.

As we read earlier in Matthew 5, the Christian life isn't meant to be lived alone and in a closet. This is where a personalized leadership development plan is so important. For the introverted or shy students in your ministry, you will need to stair-step them along in things that they're comfortable and gifted in while all the time pushing them out of their comfort zone little by little.

Remember that leadership should be a choice for them, but always have a purposeful conversation if you see something in a student that you want to challenge them with. As with any organization, the culture of your ministry will become what you celebrate. If you celebrate leadership, then it will become something that your students will desire to do.

At this point it is necessary to give a caution. As you celebrate and encourage leadership from students in your ministry, it may be a temptation for people to become prideful about their place of leadership. It could also unintentionally lead students to place more importance on their personal giftedness than on the One who gave them their gifts. You can avoid both of these by connecting their leadership and influence to a reliance on Christ and personal transformation through Him, rather than on the skills and talents of the leader. They need to understand the most important part of being a leader is their own relationship with Jesus. As Brent Crowe, vice president of Student Leadership University, says: "Leadership begins at the feet of Jesus."[6] This is a powerful statement that students must hear often as you are developing them as leaders.

With that caution behind us, let's turn our attention back to the organization of your leadership team. As the student pastor, you should personally interview each student who desires to lead. Doing this will add to the feeling of importance that you are placing on leadership and will give you an opportunity to expand your relationship with these students to a deeper level. Over time I found that it was this group of students who I began to personally disciple at a greater level. This isn't neglecting the rest of the students because you've recruited and trained your adult volunteers well. It is strategic discipleship for you because you are spending your focused discipling time with the group of students who have stepped forward and revealed a desire to do something more.

As you interview, pay close attention to things that could be challenges for them in leadership, opportunities for development, or areas of life that might keep them from leadership at that moment. This expanded relationship will also allow you to hold your student leaders to a high level of accountability. They need to understand that moving into a position of leadership comes with a higher level of responsibility and that you're going to hold them accountable to walk with Jesus. As you develop these awesome student leaders, don't keep them all to yourself. Connect their leadership and service to the church as a whole. This is healthy for two reasons: it builds within students a love for the church and desire to serve outside their peer bubble. Second, it helps the rest of the church connect to the student ministry and see the impact students are making.

Students are given many leadership opportunities outside the church: student government, school clubs, sports teams, and community involvement, to name a few. This being true, we should be more eager to provide students with leadership opportunities that connect their skills, talents, and passions to an overarching gospel-driven purpose. Leadership developed and encouraged inside the church will lead to leadership and impact outside the church, which is the ultimate destination for all your work in developing them as leaders. If all this work were just for the purpose of them being in the church building more and doing more within those walls, it would be a waste. But that's not the purpose. Your purpose in all this work is to train them and send them out. Help them understand that the leadership they've been taking on in the ministry will translate to leadership and influence everywhere else.

Your leadership development must take them to the place where they begin seeing opportunities to influence people for Jesus in every place that God takes them: the baseball team, math team, cheerleading squad, band, student government, the gas station, their part-time job, their own homes, and a million other places and groups I haven't mentioned. The real win comes when your students begin coming up with their own ideas and projects of how they can lead in their communities and even to other parts of the world. That is when you know you have someone who has grasped the idea of being a *Culture Shaping* influence, but you have to lead them there.

Discussion Questions

1. Do we currently have a leadership team of students? Are there enough opportunities for the students who want to serve and lead?

2. What are the current opportunities in our ministry for students to serve? How can we get them plugged into those areas?

3. Who are the people that stand out, adults and students, as being passionate about leadership? Who could provide the organizational structure needed to launch effective leadership teams?

Chapter 13

International Missions

ON A RECENT TRIP TO EAST ASIA, THE LORD MOVED DEEPLY IN MY heart in the area of mobilizing students to the nations. It's something I've been passionate about both as a student pastor and now as I lead the LifeWay Student team. That passion has led me to take students on international missions experiences throughout my time in the local church as well as to start LifeWay Student Ministry's first international missions ministry, which will launch in summer 2016. But that passion has been renewed and multiplied through the recent conversations I had as I sat face-to-face with missionaries and local believers from that area.

As I observed the people in the two countries and five cities I visited on this specific trip, it resounded to me over and over that those people don't need our money, our government, our American view, or us to ride in on a white horse and save the day. What they need is the gospel. Your students can, and should, be part of the army that God is raising up to take His story to the ends of the earth. A truly *Culture Shaping* ministry will provide students with an opportunity to have an international missions experience before they graduate high school.

You might be wondering why a focus on international missions is appearing here, as a part of the *Culture Shaping* element, rather than with *Kingdom Expanding*. It could have easily fit there, but I chose to include it here because nothing else moves a student to be a *Culture Shaping* influence in their own culture more than experiencing what it looks like to live in and follow Jesus in a culture that is foreign to them.

From the beginning of Scripture to the end, God's heart for the nations is clear. It's proclaimed in Genesis that through

Abraham all nations would be blessed, and in Revelation we see that God is building a people from every tribe and tongue. Evidence exists in abundance throughout the books in between. Healthy student ministries make sure that this truth is applied deeply to the hearts of their students. It's so easy for students to get stuck in their bubble. They're busy, and their lives seem very complex, especially to them. The so-called American dream lifestyle is bombarding them every day from multiple sources. All of that melts away when they are exposed to other parts of the world where they can see how believers outside of America live and come face-to-face with the lostness of our world. There's something amazing that happens when one of your students stands next to a believer in another country and both are worshipping and praying together in their own languages. Students, and adults for that matter, who experience this will come back with a desire to live a *Culture Shaping* life not just here in America, but around the world.

We've been talking a lot about shaping culture, and in light of the global discussion here I think it's appropriate to mention that there are many aspects of culture around the world that are beautiful and good. So, in an international environment I'm not saying we need to go in and Americanize everything or even American-Christianize everything. Culture is extremely important to people. For many it is their identity and heritage, and they take great pride in who they are. To go into any situation where people are not like you and attempt to change their culture would be a mistake.

This point was made clear in a recent conversation I had with a missionary about Revelation 7:9, where John witnessed the multitude from every nation, tribe, and tongue. When John looked at this multitude, he immediately knew they were from every nation and tribe. This missionary's argument was that there must have been some physical appearance that caused him to see their differences immediately: faces, colors, the way they dressed, the tribal markings that may have been on some, etc. The point is that if John was seeing these stark cultural differences in his view of heaven, then culture is not only important to people of this earth, but also different cultures are important to God.

The story of Daniel is a great illustration of what it means to be a culture shaper in this context. The story begins with Daniel, a Hebrew, being taken into captivity by the Babylonians. He was thrust into their culture immediately because he was seen as someone with a lot of potential who could serve in the king's court. He was trained in their language, their history, their art, and belief systems. He was given a crash course in Babylonian culture, and for the most part he adhered to what he was being taught. He embraced much of the culture in which he found himself, except for a few areas. We see throughout Daniel's life, and the lives of his friends, that he stood against the culture any time the culture went against His belief in the one true God. He didn't belittle their history or belief system, even though it was pagan in nature. Instead, he lived in their culture and was a clear influence for God. He was a *Culture Shaping* influence, even to the king himself, and didn't go into the new culture with a metaphorical hammer and tear it all down. In general, we as Americans should be much more accepting of other cultures of the world, including here in our own country. After all, we will be worshipping with them in heaven one day if not here on earth through some missions experience.

Leading a *Culture Shaping* ministry will mean that you have students in your ministry currently and ones who have graduated from it who are *Culture Shaping* students. Part of being a *Culture Shaping* student is having God's heart for the nations. This leads us to two very important questions. The first is: How can I introduce my students to God's heart for the nations? It is a continual process. It has to be something that touches every part of your ministry in some way.

God's heart for the nations isn't transferred merely through a program or a trip. It has to begin with you as the student pastor and your volunteer leadership team and flow into the students from there. Practically speaking, here are some things you must do if your students are going to have God's heart for the nations:

1. Preach the gospel clearly at every opportunity. As people come to understand more about the gospel—what it is, how to share it, how it has changed

them—the natural progression is to develop God's heart for people.

2. Spend time focusing on what God is doing in other parts of the world. This information is easy to find through the Internet and sending organizations like the International Mission Board.

3. Connect with missionaries who can share and give a firsthand account of how God is working and using them on the mission field. In many cases this is a great opportunity to begin a relationship with specific missionaries in an area of the world where you can have an ongoing partnership in the work they're doing. This also helps you avoid the temptation to go on missioncation, the practice of choosing a location in the world you would really like to visit and then trying to find a mission opportunity there. That's the wrong motivation, and your students will see right through it. Get to know the culture, the people groups, and the missionaries involved in the area of the world you are interested in working.

4. Give your students opportunities to go on mission trips. As I mentioned earlier, every student should have the opportunity to go on an international missions experience before they graduate high school. Exhaust your efforts to try and find a way to take students off of American soil. If you can't find a way, or want an option for younger students, there are several cities within the United States that are refugee centers where you can have an international missions experience without ever leaving our soil.

5. Encourage your students to take seriously the learning of a language other than English in high school. This is something I completely missed as a student pastor and that I've been convicted about in recent days. Most schools require students to take a foreign language, and if it isn't a requirement they are still offered as elective options. Language is a barrier to sharing the gospel around the world and if we are truly going to be part of the mobilization team that sends *Culture Shaping* students to the ends of the earth to share the

gospel, then we should encourage them to learn a language rather than take some throwaway elective that will never matter.

The second question is: What does it look like for a student to have God's heart for the nations? I struggled with answering this question for you because I've been so against any kind of spiritual checklist to this point, but I'm going to answer it out of a desire to be extremely practical in the application of this chapter. I'm going to give you things that I have seen in students personally as they've grown in their understanding of God's heart for the nations, and as a result of how all these things fit together, these qualities are also present and growing in students who I would say are *Culture Shaping* students.

1. They understand and can articulate the gospel.
2. They understand that the gospel is meant to reach beyond them and their immediate circle.
3. They have predetermined to say yes to God in whatever He calls them to do or wherever He calls them to go.

4. They begin to care less about the things of this world because their gaze is becoming more and more fixed on Jesus.

5. They begin to use the platforms God has given them in their daily lives as opportunities to share the gospel.

6. They become less and less content with what many (unfortunately) may see as normal Christianity.

7. They will want to bring others along with them in their pursuit of taking Jesus to the ends of the earth.

8. They will want to go to the nations, and if that isn't possible they will find a way to be connected to what God is doing around the world.

One word of caution as you begin to consider your ministry's international missions involvement: avoid "missioncation." This is a common practice where the leadership and/or students pick a place they've never been but think would be really cool to visit, and then plan a missions experience there. The next year the trip is in a different place, and that pattern stays the same for every year that a student is involved in your missions efforts. While this makes for an awesome-looking passport, a much more healthy approach is to find a place, or even a few places, that you are involved with frequently. This way you are teaching your students the value of Kingdom partnerships while at the same time helping them see the long-term impact that's being made in a region or with a specific people group. Your students will have opportunities to build relationships with people from the places that you visit, which often results in the heart of a student being more drawn to the mission of God than in the missioncation model.

I know there are many of you who have never been on an international missions experience and may feel a little awkward about this chapter as a result. There are probably many of you who want to do something like this but look around at your church and the resources available and it seems like a really daunting task. Others of you are about to plan a trip right now so you can drop off the squirrelly kid from your ministry we mentioned earlier. All that is to say, if there's no international missions focus happening in your ministry right now, that's okay. But don't stay there. Start something. The first thing you do doesn't have to be a trip to the other side of the world, unless the Lord calls you. Choose today to begin revealing God's heart for the nations to each and every student in your ministry.

Discussion Questions

1. Do we give our students enough opportunities to be involved in an international missions experience?

2. What are the steps we need to take to get more students in our ministry involved internationally?

3. What are some things we can do right away to help more students connect with God's heart for the nations?

Why Did I Get into This?

HAVE YOU EVER ASKED YOURSELF THIS QUESTION? AS A STUDENT pastor or volunteer leader, have you ever just stopped, looked around, and wondered why in the world you got into ministering to students? If so, you're not alone, and it doesn't mean you're a horrible leader. It means you're in student ministry.

I've asked this question many times through the years; and while it never gets any easier to answer, it is a question worth answering. Sometimes when people face this question they run, like I did in the beginning. I ran because I didn't want to doubt my calling, and I ran because I was afraid I couldn't come up with an answer. For others it's dismissed immediately and pushed out of their minds. But by answering this question through the years I've learned a valuable lesson: wrestling with this question isn't meant to cripple you, it's meant to strengthen you. Here's how:

1. It brings you back to the things God has done in your life personally.
2. It brings you back to how God has worked through you in the ministry.
3. It builds your faith.
4. It matures you personally and as a minister.
5. It refines your vision for ministry.
6. It helps you remember your calling.

There are many different answers to this question that change based on circumstances, but there really is only one answer. You got into this because God called you to it.

It isn't something that man called you to do, or that you woke up one morning declaring. God called you to pastor students and their families. This is something that should bring you great confidence. Stop and think for a moment about the truth that God has specifically set you apart and shaped you to minister to a group of students. There may be times when you feel like you aren't supported in your role. There may be times when you feel like no one thinks you can do it, and there may be times when even you don't believe you can. The reality is that God called you to student ministry.

Don't listen to the naysayers, and don't listen to yourself in times of doubt. Get alone with the Lord and dwell upon His goodness and His provision in your calling. Look at Paul's encouragement to the elders at the church of Ephesus in Acts 20:28: "Be on guard for yourselves and for all the flock that the Holy Spirit has appointed you to as overseers, to shepherd the church of God, which He purchased with His own blood." There's a lot happening in this passage that we could talk through, but I want to focus you specifically to the phrase "for all the flock that the Holy Spirit has appointed you to as overseers, to shepherd the church of God." Have you ever thought about the fact that God has appointed you to shepherd the students that are in your ministry?

He appointed you, not someone else who may be a better speaker or group leader, or someone who has more resources to give. In His sovereignty He placed you in the role you're in so that you can disciple a group of students and their families. If God has appointed you to your group of students, then the reverse of that statement is also true: God has appointed those students to you. You are the one He picked, for this time, to be a spiritual influence in their lives. If you are a volunteer small-group leader, you don't have the group you have by accident. God divinely matched you up.

As you dwell on God's goodness and provision in your calling, it builds a needed Christ-centered confidence. Here are seven things you can be confident about because of God's call on your life:

1. God's call outweighs man's call every time.
2. Focusing on God's call takes you out of the spotlight.
3. When God calls you, He equips you.

4. Ministry is done through Christ's strength, not yours.
5. God's call is an anchor during times of doubt.
6. Because of God's call, you aren't in student ministry alone.
7. God will always be at work in you and in your ministry.

It still blows me away to think about how God specifically set me apart for ministry. There was nothing that earned me that calling. Instead, God chose me and equipped me out of His love and grace. The same is true for you. When people doubt you, when you doubt yourself, remember that you got into this because God called you to it.

My prayer for you as a leader in student ministry is that your ministry would be healthy, that it would be *Kingdom Expanding, Character Transforming,* and *Culture Shaping,* and that you would lead your ministry in the strength God provides and in the Christ-centered confidence His calling on your life will bring.

About the Author

BEN TRUEBLOOD SERVES AS THE DIRECTOR OF STUDENT MINISTRY for LifeWay Christian Resources and has served the local church as a student pastor for fourteen years. In addition to his role at LifeWay, Ben is involved in training, consulting, and speaking to student ministries throughout the U.S. Ben and his wife, Kristen, have four young children and reside in Nashville, Tennessee.

Notes

1. A. N. Wilson, *Tolstoy: A Biography* (New York: W. W. Norton and Company, 2011).

2. John Stott, *The Cross of Christ* (Downers Grove, IL: InterVarsity Press, 2006).

3. Andy Reinhardt, *Business Week* (May 1998), www.businessweek.com/1998/21/b3579165.html.

4. See www.georgehguthrie.com.

5. Wayne Grudem, *Systematic Theology* (Downers Grove, IL: InterVarsity Press, 1994), 29.

6. Brent Crowe, *Sacred Intent* (Franklin, TN: Worthy Publishing, 2015), 23.

IF YOU ENJOYED THIS BOOK,
WILL YOU CONSIDER SHARING IT WITH OTHERS?

• Grab copies for your volunteer team and read it with them utilizing the discussion questions.

• Recommend the book to your student ministry friends, your local student ministry network, or others on your church staff.

• Mention the book in a blog post or through social media using the hashtag #studentministrythatmatters.

• Go to **facebook.com/Ben.R.Trueblood**, "Like" the page, and engage in further student ministry conversation.

• Twitter: "If you're interested in leading a healthy student ministry I recommend reading #studentministrythatmatters by @bentrueblood"

• Write a book review online.

WAYS TO CONNECT WITH BEN TRUEBLOOD:

WEBSITE: BENTRUEBLOOD.COM
TWITTER: @BENTRUEBLOOD
FACEBOOK: FACEBOOK.COM/BEN.R.TRUEBLOOD